CRIPTALES

To request an accessible version
of this book, please contact
access@nickhernbooks.co.uk

CRIPTALES

Six Monologues

Curated by
Mat Fraser

NICK HERN BOOKS
London
www.nickhernbooks.co.uk

A Nick Hern Books

CripTales first published in Great Britain in 2020 as a paperback original by Nick Hern Books Limited, The Glasshouse, 49a Goldhawk Road, London W12 8QP, by arrangement with the BBC, and in association with the BBC Studios production *CripTales*

Designed and typeset by Nick Hern Books, London

Printed in the UK by Mimeo Ltd, Huntingdon, Cambridgeshire PE29 6XX

A CIP catalogue record for this book is available from the British Library

ISBN 978 1 84842 985 7

Contents

Introduction
Mat Fraser, Creative Director

When I was growing up as a young disabled boy in a mainstream, wholly able-bodied school, the whole world seemed able-bodied. I didn't know any other disabled people, let alone kids my age. At that time, television was reinforcing the notion that we pretty much didn't exist, and when we did, it was generally pitiful.

The only two exceptions to this in the 1970s were the blind teacher in the exotic series *Kung Fu*, and Sandy the receptionist from the less-exotic soap *Crossroads*. Neither actor was really disabled, of course, but they both had characters that at least had self-respect – and a job. Yet I felt no affinity with them, for so many reasons. It's relevant that the writers were not disabled.

In the intervening years, disabled people's rights have been enshrined into law, and attitudes have changed for the better. Jobs in the dramatic arts, however, have continued to be few and far between for disabled writers, directors and actors. It is improving, but ill-informed versions of disability, written and portrayed by non-disabled people, still abound in mainstream screen output.

Even now, in 2020, there is a plethora of stories and experiences from a disabled perspective that have been left untold, unspoken, and about which most people have no idea. A perfect opportunity then to follow the BBC's excellent television series *Queers* and *Snatches* – which featured monologues by and about, respectively, the gay and female experience – with *CripTales*, a series of monologues about the disabled experience, written by disabled writers.

With six slots to fill, and over twenty impairment groups (off the top of my head) needing exposure, doing it by impairment was clearly not going to work! A different approach was needed. Debbie Christie, the executive producer, and I took time to compile a list of good disabled writers, from personal knowledge, disability databases, Graeae Theatre Company's excellent training programme for writers, and others who had been through similar BBC schemes.

The shocking lack of screenwriting opportunities for these writers, most of whom were more than experienced enough to take on such work, told us that these monologues were so needed, to reveal authentic disabled voices talking about disabled experiences. Diversity was, of course, paramount as we set forth, aware that the voices of disabled women, disabled people of colour, and disabled gay people, were all perspectives that have been particularly unheard and unseen. With all the writers, we first asked what they might want to write, given our remit of wanting the monologues to reflect something to do with disability in the last fifty or so years.

Sex and disability, especially when containing procreation or prevention, is something of a rarity in writing, from anyone. Genevieve Barr is a deaf writer and actor, and after reading her writing, we eagerly met her and were enthused by her intention to tell a story about abortion. Set against the law permitting abortion in the UK, in 1968, *Thunderbox* is a powerful and emotional piece: a direct, personal and complex study of disability, abortion, religion, and social pressures. This is a perfect example of the stories that TV audiences have previously not had access to, that can only enrich our understanding of disability and humanity.

Thankfully, all the writers had clear ideas of what they wanted to write. For myself, an older disabled male actor and writer, a funny and sharp look at years of the audition process was what I wanted to expose, thoroughly deconstruct, and poke fun at. I juxtaposed it with my own life experiences, which have led me to be what I am. Thus, *Audition* is honest, pulls no kicks (I don't punch), and speaks directly to the screen industry. I may never get another acting job again!

Becoming disabled is a trope often used by able-bodied writers. Usually wrong, tragic, ill-informed and embarrassing to most disabled people, it's something hardly ever seen written *by* disabled people. With her career in performance poetry and her experiences of housing-estate life in the North of England, Jackie Hagan came to us with the freshest of disabled women's voices. Another first-time TV screenwriter who has been writing for over ten years, her piece, *Paper Knickers*, is unflinching, direct, ultra-personal, yet also a romantic and hopeful look at acquiring an impairment. Like myself, Jackie performed her own piece, and our two monologues are the most personal of the six stories.

Matilda Ibini became know to us as a black disabled woman with such a fresh voice. Her idea of exploring the power dynamic of carers and their disabled 'clients', from a gay black disabled woman's perspective, was radically different, and something we eagerly commissoned her to write. *The Shed* is Matilda's first TV writing to be screened.

Commissioning Jack Thorne was a must! Probably the most famous disabled writer of screen work in the world, his name would ensure much-needed attention, and we knew he could deliver a fantastic piece of drama. We were thrilled when he immediately agreed to write a monologue, despite his ridiculously busy schedule. Jack's idea of a story about a gay man getting his first electric wheelchair, and the freedom that allows, during 1981's 'Year of the Disabled', was perfect, and he was duly given a green light to go ahead. He ended up writing a beautiful, poignant, funny and rude piece, working with Robert Softley Gale, a well-known gay disabled actor and director from Scotland, who performed the piece, *Hamish*, brilliantly.

Tom Wentworth is an example of a professional disabled writer never handed the reins. He's a seasoned participant of many disability writing schemes, working on existing returning series, but not given the opportunity to write what he wanted and get it screened. It was a joy to receive his idea of a benefits fraudster helping a genuine disabled person receive her benefits. Disability rights and wrongs in one piece, a shifting perspective as it develops, cheeky as hell, and a much-needed comment on the current and often dire situation so many British disabled people are in. A difficult subject, written with great humour, *The Real Deal* is a roller-coaster of a story, with a sting in its tail…

Is *CripTales* the tip of the disability iceberg? You bet! But it's a great start, I hope you'll agree, and a wonderful place for disabled writers to take control of their stories. My hope is that it will lead to more and more television production companies looking for authentic voices and stories about disability and – who knows? – even allow us to write stories that contain all of humanity, ourselves included.

THUNDERBOX

Genevieve Barr

First performed by **Ruth Madeley**
as part of the BBC Studios Scotland production *CripTales*
on BBC America and BBC Four, directed by Amit Sharma.

The Abortion Act was passed in 1967.

The whole monologue takes place in a Portaloo – what they used to call a 'thunderbox' – at a music festival during the summer of 1968.

At the festival, The Seekers are performing 'Georgy Girl'. SUE *sits on the loo, tights around her ankles, knitting as she sings along to the first verse.*

Jack Kelly walked into my granddad's bed shop and asked if he could buy a mattress. I was sat at the counter, reading my *Lady Penelope* and when he saw me, he said he'd have me on top of it an' all. The mattress. Not my *Lady Penelope*. My jaw just...

But then he laughed and it was so... joyous, before me granddad heard him and went after him with a Dial-A-Matic. Thankfully it weren't worse, he were watching over the butcher shop next door!

So I put my jaw back up. And that was that, you know. Or at least I thought it was. He came back the next day. I was just... Never thought a boy like that would look at me – like that – and just be like – (*Shrugs.*) Okay. Not special like. Just... okay. Okay's fine with me.

SUE *smiles to herself.*

We had our first date at the bed shop. 'Why go elsewhere when we have all we need for romance here?' he said. I'm not one to argue. I locked up and span around with my hands on my hips like I'd seen my nan do in her dancing classes. 'Where are the candles then?' He said. Not that we did candles. They don't really mix well with goose eiderdown. He got us a pie and I let him have some whisky.

Ten years, ten years younger and all the spaces between us. It din't matter. We didn't touch. He said he stank of wool from working at the docks. But there was a magnetism in our minds. I flustered at its simple promise.

She gives us a look, sizing us up.

My ma had a backstreet abortion. They gave her a choice. It were 'Farrer's Catholic Pills' or a quick jab up – there – with the needles. She chose the pills.

Didn't do the job. Hospitalised her, barely survived. She said she wouldn't wish the pain on anyone. Worse than childbirth… doesn't sound right that? When I arrived, three years later all crooked, she said I were punishment for her sins.

Someone hammers at the door.

Alright, pipe down! Let a lady go about her business.

She takes a sip of a not-before-seen drink. Very debonair. She resumes knitting.

Sex was… I once walked in on my nan blowing the hairdryer up on her – box. Her face… it were like a cross between when she's found a corner piece of her jigsaw – and when my ma occasionally comes home and tries to fob off with her baccy. This peculiar, reluctant delight.

It were the first time she swore at me. 'You've got hands! Yer can bloody knock!' I just stood there. 'Won't you burn yourself?' I asked. She pressed her lips. Tightly. Like she was trying to squash a smile. 'All things need a bit of an airing from time to time.' I could barely breathe for crying with laughter.

'Best to get it done quick.' He said. First time won't feel like our minds meeting. 'And then you'll start to blossom!' 'Blossom? What? Like a cocoon?' His voice sounded funny. 'A cocoon?' He said. 'A cockoon.' I replied. He laughed and – his skin smelt nice. They'd been loading Cheshire salts on the boats at the docks.

She sings the second verse of 'Georgy Girl'.

She takes a deep breath. It's not pain but it's discomfort.

Her hands shake again. She firmly knits a new stitch in what is starting to look like a baby booty.

My granddad got the bizzies involved. 'It weren't right,' they all said. So they went calling for him down at the docks. Granddad dragged me down and all, in case he didn't come by his name. I remembered how our minds met. He was gone. Dockmaster said:'He's a woollyback – what'd we expect?!' Then – 'Girl like her'll be grateful.' Granddad didn't need his Dial-A-Matic that time.

Pain hits her. She waits for it to subside.

Doctors described me to my ma as subnormal. That was the word.

'You've got a girl but I'm afraid she's come out subnormal.' Polite.

They said, given the outcome had been... unexpected, no one would judge if – if things didn't work – out. Community care could be arranged. They could fix to have us sterilised. It might be kind. Kinder. That's British eugenics for you! My nan put a stop to all that.

Fourteen, I were knitting baby clothes for Barnardo's to send over to the colonies. Ma walked in and oh. She didn't like that at all.

Snatched them, right out my hand. Pulled the stitches out. No. No more. She said. You're the end of the line.

I tried to kiss her and lick the whisky from her breath. Babies need to be kept warm. Helps them feel safe.

She dabs a tissue between her legs and finds blood.

My ma drove me. In Granddad's car. My nan... couldn't. Three hundred miles away. A small cottage hospital. My ma stayed in the car. 'You've got to get rid,' she said. 'It's not right.'

Slipped me bus fare, lit up a fag and shot off in a plume of smoke.

I sat in the disappointment room. Last on the list. 'It might get more complicated with you.' I got a pat on the hand. They went in. They went out. A lady whispered: 'You're lucky, you know. No one's going to judge you for getting rid.' Got another pat.

My turn, I went in, doctor said: 'You've made the right choice.' He...

She pats her own hand.

I felt my legs pick me up and carry me away.

She dabs a tissue between her legs and finds blood again. She closes her legs again carefully. She sniffles.

When I got back, Nan was knitting by the fire. She knew. I said I'm having her! Nan cried. Said she was too old. No. No more. Not again. Who's to raise her? Me! I said. You're not fit. She said. Me! I can do it! I can! Her lips pressed tightly. For a long time. Then she patted me on the hand and said – 'Be fair. Life's not fair.'

She almost verbally explodes. She stutters on a precipice as she tries to articulate what she wants to say.

Then she restrains herself and the tears – but it's the hardest thing she's done.

The – the point is – Father, I wanted her. Will you let her know that, please?

She sobs.

We see, on the tip of the knitting needles, there is blood. Her voice then takes on this soporific quality.

'And the Lord spoke to Moses and said, "None of your offspring throughout their generations with a blemish may approach to offer the bread of his God."'

White eyelashes. White eyebrows. White hair. A heart. A heartbeat. My angel delight. Forgive me, Father. Forgive me, darling girl.

She sits there, motionless, bloody knitting needles in her hands.

Fade to black.

AUDITION

Mat Fraser

First performed by **Mat Fraser**
as part of the BBC Studios Scotland production *CripTales*
on BBC America and BBC Four, directed by Ewan Marshall.

Dramaturg, April De Angelis

MAT, *intimate, close, soft.*

'I look old to you, yeah? Well, older, I know I do. I am, so I must do. There's no space to see the full picture, so you're concentrating on my face. Have a good long look…'

(With a different delivery.) *'I look old to you, yeah? Well, older, I know I do. I am, so I must…'*

Ah.

Auditions, are for me, the single most nerve-racking aspect of acting. More terrifying than a first night on stage, or a first scene on a new set. Like most actors I can't control getting the part, just the acting.

But, unlike most actors, not getting the part can often have nothing to do with my acting, and everything to do with, these.

He stands up so his hands become the only things on screen. He screams loudly.

AAARRGGGHHHH!

He sits back down.

These babies, over the last twenty-five years, have caused commotions, disruptions, shame even. Oh not for me, I love the power of my magic hands. I love my body. No, really, I do. It is the only one I've got.

'Thou, nature, art my goddess. To thy law
My services are bound. Wherefore should I
Stand in the plague of custom and permit
The curiosity of nations to deprive me?'

I used to do Edmund's speech from *King Lear*, but it all got a bit self-reffy, you know? Like, yes Edmund dude, I hear you loud and clear, and so do the 2004 casting director and director…

'What a cunning choice, ha, he's speaking about himself in society, through a Shakespearean character, how lovely, clever too. Mmm...'

No.

I got here too early – it's better than being too late, that's worse. Anything that causes more tension in the room counts against my getting the job. I say 'more' because it's often already quite tense in there.

'What if he sees me staring at his hands?'

'What if he's crap and I find it embarrassing?'

'What if we fumble the greeting handshake? – Oh God, the handshake.'

'What if the audience can't believe him in the role?'

'What if I can't believe him in the role, because his body looks weird, his body isn't normal, his body, his body, his body body body bod bod bod bod bo bo bo b b b – BAM!'

My flippers intervened. POW! My hands got shaken in between, your very practised smile, and the normal I defiled.

SLAM! Dunked in your expectations, my refreshing permutations.

I'm going to go in there, ignore all that crap in my head, and do my best acting performance, so I can leave with my head held high and with self-respect, if not with the job...

But, the job's the thing, the only thing, worth having, from this. I certainly don't do it so they can have their first experience of auditioning, then passing on, a disabled actor.

This one's a real, actual part. I mean, one of two characters involved in the central narrative, school sweethearts that meet again on Skype after thirty years because somebody died on Facebook. It'd be brilliant!

So many ways it could go wrong.

Open door, smile and close door with glib ease for their relief and comfort. Approach desk and pretend not to notice as they all try really hard to only look at your face with partial success. Possibly take off coat and put down bag, make it look good, don't fumble, they read it as nerves, which makes them nervous.

Look bright and breezy smiling as they ask usually the same obligatory two or three questions:

'How did you get here?'

'How is your agent?'

'Do you know a random disabled actor that they didn't give a job to five years ago?'

'Yes, I think I do know them, ha, lovely guy.'

Huh, I can just see them, sitting there by that scary desk of authority. Casting people, director, producer.

That, desk, such a physical barrier, protecting their ancient normality rituals – I want to get on top of it, squat down and take a profound dump right there, so they can see their own steaming prejudice in all its hateful glory. That probably wouldn't, work.

I'm beginning to sweat, my heart rate's too fast, I'm in a state of anxiety. Damn! I'm even starting to question my clothing choice – This says long-lost lover, right? I've got to get a grip. Harder with no thumbs, but not impossible...

When I was twelve, Mr Proctor our fashionable English teacher who I loved because I thought that he liked me, asked us to write a narrated version of a famous fairytale. I wrote a version of *Goldilocks and the Three Bears*, describing an imaginary Goldilocks, and had three mates miming the bears.

When they saw Goldilocks sleeping, Baby Bear said: *'Look!'* Mummy Bear said: *'Oh my!'* But then I had Daddy Bear do his own line: *'Phwooaar!'* Mr Proctor roared, and I was hooked, for life, to the Best Drug in the World: audience appreciation.

In that moment I didn't feel like the only disabled kid in the school, I felt wanted, appreciated, valued. And it made Carol Anne laugh. Next term, Mr Proctor announced the school play.

I rushed up to him and eagerly announced my intention to audition, expecting his typically warm and generous response. Instead, I got an alarming fixed smile.

'…Great!'

On the day I waited for my turn to audition. Carol Anne was sitting at the back of the hall, and I looked forward to impressing her with my acting performance… Mr Proctor looked so nervous, and then as I looked up and out with confidence as I'd been taught at home, I saw Carol Anne laughing. She looked embarrassed. It drilled into my skull like self-hating trepanation.

How's this for a character breakdown?

'Father, fifty, could be disabled.'

Never seen that. Never. I have on my lucky underwear briefs, stripy ones that are fraying but I've got three jobs in them and, now ten years old, are reserved for auditions.

There's a small hole where my ball skin sometimes gets painfully trapped near the leg elastic, but it's usually worth the risk.

Four minutes to go, feeling okay. Should I gesticulate during it, so they can see what that looks like, or would it put them off? Perhaps I should do a task so they can see I can 'manage'? I once lit a cigarette in an audition but really badly, and the lighter burned my eyebrow which everybody saw but pretended not to notice. Didn't get that job. Eyebrow grew back after a couple of months.

Maybe I could slightly flirt with one of them so they can see I've got that kind of traditional man, sexuality and charisma. That too hasn't gone well historically. Even worse with women.

For a while back there, all six of us UK male disabled actors, ages spanning twenty-five years, would get called in for the same audition.

'Hi, I don't know if I'm meant to be here, it says that the role's for a character with CP?'

'Well, if you could read the lines anyway, and try to portray cerebral palsy?'

(In a 'CP voice'.) 'I need help on the toilet.'

'Wow! That was amazing. So, moving.'

No, it's not amazing, it's not even acting, it's mimicry, nothing more. Don't get angry, Mat. Leave it outside the room. You don't want to get a reputation for being disabled and 'difficult'.

Worst audition? I got one for a new musical about Italian castrati, and I was out of my depth. I chose to sing 'The Age of Aquarius'. The look on their faces as I entered the room, told me that my agent had not informed them of my glorious physique, and it took them a while to remember that I could see them as well as they could see me, and alter their facial contortions accordingly. This should have told me *'Get out, now!'* – but no, I handed my sheet music to the facially supportive pianist, undermining the last of my confidence with his look of *'Poor man, he'll never make it'* and launched into my high-energy rendition of the rock-musical classic.

MAT *sings, a cappella, 'The Age of Aquarius' from* Hair.

I worked the room, moving through the space as if singing it on stage, as all three jaws slowly dropped as one to my high-spirited performance.

I finished. There was silence as three open-mouthed conservative musical-theatre toughies, all looked blank, then shut their cakeholes...

'Thank you, Mat, for that. Thank you, that was, uh... Thanks!'

My hands are the work of the devil for some people. I've got short arms as a result of my mum taking Thalidomide, a morning-sickness drug.

'It says on your résumé that you have prosthetic arms, do you ever use them?'

Alternating shots with and without prosthetic arms.

(*With*.) I won't get the job because they don't want to send the wrong message.

(*Without*.) I will get the job cos the real message is that there's no message.

(*With*.) Because disabled actors cannot be bad guys.

(*Without*.) Because it's interesting casting for a bad guy.

(*With*.) Because the casting agent is scared of what the director might say.

(*Without*.) Because the casting agent has resolve, and the director lives in the present century.

An arm drops out of sleeve.

Then the after-care emails, to really drive home the point they don't even know they're making:

'You didn't get it, sorry, but they were really glad you came in.'

'You didn't get it, sorry, but they really liked your performance.'

'You didn't get it, sorry, but they said how much you brought to the role.'

'I checked in with casting and you got some really lovely feedback on your self-tape. They were really happy and excited about it. You didn't get it, sorry.'

All those roles that could have been. All that audience understanding, achieved, that equality, imagined, career highlights... Spilt milk.

Aged seven, my mum took me somewhere official, I could feel it in her air, she kept looking away. We sat down in a waiting room. Opposite and around me were loads of kids with short arms, I'd never seen anyone that looked like me before. They called my name, but Mum wasn't allowed to come in with me. When I entered the room I saw, behind a scary desk of authority, three men in suits, smiling who said *'Come and sit in the chair opposite.'* They asked me questions.

'Everything alright?'

'How's school?'

'Do you know any of the random children outside?'

Then, one of them told me that in the top drawer of a filing cabinet, stood about five feet tall, was loads of candy, and chocolate, and that I could just help myself. So I got up, clutched the chair, dragged it over to the filing cabinet, stood on top of the chair so I could reach, opened the drawer, got a bar of chocolate out, shut the drawer and jumped back off the chair. The three men looked at each other, and the one in the middle, wearing a pinstripe double-breasted suit holding open an ink pen, wrote 'fifteen thousand pounds'.

I'd just been means-tested by the people that deformed me. A compensation assessment by the drug company. They didn't ask me to tie up a shoelace, or do up my top button, or lots of things, on purpose. I passed their audition but I failed myself.

Had I known that audition was a means test, I would have chin-crawled my way across the floor, bitten my agonising way up the filing cabinet, and then failed to get any chocolate. I might have been only seven, but I'm the son of two actors, for God's sake.

Yes... I am. It's in my blood, in my heart, filling my head, with calm, assurance. I'm going to go into that audition room, and wow them with a great acting performance, and convince them that I, am the right actor for the part, short arms, flipper hands, no thumbs and all...

VOICE OFF-CAMERA. Mat?

MAT. Yup.

Fade to black.

PAPER KNICKERS

Jackie Hagan

First performed by **Jackie Hagan**
as part of the BBC Studios Scotland production *CripTales*
on BBC America and BBC Four, directed by Ewan Marshall.

STACY HADFIELD.

Why give *me* this choice? I don't make decisions, my life's just happened to me. I was born, not my choice, and then school just happens at ya, 'the ink is black, the page is white, together we learn to' snog with gobs full of cider and resentment, and then what? I got older, I couldn't help it, I started wearing lipstick and shouting and now it's now and I'm sat on a hospital bed waiting for a porter to wheel me to a completely different life.

They said something about blood clots, they can travel from your leg up into your brain, or it might have been your heart, can't be your heart, too weird, too poetic. Too embarrassed to tell 'em I wasn't listening. Doctors innit, they're like policemen or teachers, doesn't feel like a conversation just feels like big dog, little dog and I'm a chihuahua.

God I can't focus with all this beeping! Sounds like a techno album that doesn't know how to dance. I've already signed the form to say chop my leg off. I didn't really think about it I just agreed with the doctor.

Do you know what I do when I'm faced with something life-changing?

I do nothing. When my dad sloped off out the door on Christmas Day with a bottle of whisky and a badly packed suitcase there was only me who saw him go, he winked at me, full of guilt that wink, and I said nothing, I did nothing. I went back into the living room and unwrapped my Christmas present and it was a pogo stick. I've hated them ever since.

I've got loads of 'Get Well' cards.

She opens one.

'Get well soon from Gaz.'

She rips it up.

She opens another one.

'Best wishes, Karen.'

She rips it up.

No one knows what to say.

'Get Well'? I'm in hospital riddled with blood clots, not seven years old with a cold watching *Fantasia* while me mum makes me a chucky egg! I'm not gonna get well. Neither option is about being well. If I go through with it. No one'll want to talk to me cos they'll be scared of saying the word 'leg'.

Why is it embarrassing, it's like wearing a wig isn't it, it's embarrassing because we're all pretending that it's real hair, and it might fall off or something.

If I don't let them cut it off then I'd have to live with the pain. Spend the rest of my days smashed off my head on morphine watching *Homes Under the Hammer* and falling asleep to *Countdown*. What was I gonna do with my life anyway?

Sounds ace doesn it, being off your tree all day on free drugs all day, but drugs are only good if you get to be *not* on them sometimes.

You lose yourself, on morphine. There are bits of my personality I would like to lose, I'm dead clumsy in my mind, I'll say anything, I was having it off with this lad one time and at the crucial moment I said to him: 'Ooh hang on... we've got that cup in work.' I don't know if I would like to get rid of that bit. I like being ridiculous. It's important.

What bits of your personality are stored in your right leg? At least it's far away from me, my leg is as far away from me on me that you can get, if it was closer, like in my head, toothache or earache, then that'd be well worse. Plus, people love symmetry, people freak out if something's a bit wrong. If I had one leg I wouldn't be symmetrical. I'd be unshaggable. And what's unshaggable, unloveable.

Susan Matthews. She's not dead fit or anything. She goes in The Dog and Gun. I've talked at her. A bit of my tooth came out and

I didn't go out that night cos I thought how could someone like her like someone with dodgy teeth? All I wanna do is impress her. So far I've been a proper weirdo, my particular brand of flirting is a delicate mix of push-up bras and bullying but with Susan Matthews I just lost it, I was trying to flirt and I kept doing a shit Irish accent by mistake, she's not even Irish I'd just been watching *The Commitments* the night before. I panicked and I drew two eyes on my hand and I went: 'Do you not fancy a threesome?'

I dunno know why she's got me a card when I'm such an utter dickhead. If it's got flowers on the front then that just means that she's picked up the first one that she could find, but if it's an arty one, like a kitten in a big cup or a frog mid-jump then that means she's put, you know, a bit more effort into it.

It's properly disabled having one leg, isn't it? Like you've been to war, or you own a motorbike.

What if they cut it off and then it doesn't heal and then they have to cut more off and then that doesn't heal, and do they keep going until I'm just a head? They'd make a documentary about me then, wouldn't they? Fame and fortune but you're just a head.

I don't want the 'aww' factor. All sing-song lilt and tilt of the head 'awwwww are you in a wheelchair? Do you want me to take that pint off of you?' 'No I pissing don't.'

Maybe it would be easier to be assertive to a porter. Porters are nice dad-shaped men. Doctors are skinny and scary. No. I've already got paper knickers on. You can't go back once you've got paper knickers on. They've drawn a big arrow on my leg. Felt too intimate, drawing on you in felt tip like your best mate would. Maybe I caused this. Maybe living off lager, lard, Angel Delight and repressed class rage isn't good for your veins.

Who needs Susan Matthews anyway, paying lip service getting me a card when I've made such a show of myself? Big deal, she's probably just kind. If we got together I couldn't be me, I'd have to buy a blouse. She probably grows her own herbs and thinks that's normal. God, I hate people.

That word: 'stump'. Stump. Stupid frump. Couldn't let anyone see. She's all pink eyeshadow and books.

She opens Susan's card.

She's drawn it herself. She's drawn me, but I look nice. And I've got a false leg. 'Stop trying to impress me. I was impressed from the start.'

The shame of it.

Someone injects her hand via a cannula.

You can tell, in here, the patients who are greyscale, smoking their fingers to the bone, and the other ones in full colour, doing word searches in new pyjamas, same problems, but they're loved. That's the difference. All you need is love.

No it's not. Excuse me! Excuse me, no one's listening. I've changed my mind. It's just, it's not very feasible for me at this time, am I gonna have my leg off because I'm too scared to be assertive? I'll be alright, won't I?

Hospital. It is three years later, and she has a false leg.

When I left the hospital they gave me a list of things to avoid, and one of them was falling over. Every taxi driver tells me that I could be a Paralympian. Aye mate, and you could be an Olympian, couldn't ya?

I get called inspirational every five minutes just for anything, just for like eating a Twix. And every day I get asked if it hurts to have your leg cut off, I use all my powers of language to sum up the pain, and it's this: 'You know when you stub your toe? Well piss off.'

Getting disability benefits was a joke, and I couldn't get a ground-floor flat, so I lived in a van for a bit, nearly froze to death, it took a while to heal, my stump, oh and I got over myself about the word 'stump'! I love it now, I'll show you what I've done with it in a bit...

I found out what bits of your personality are stored in your right leg. I stopped feeling ashamed for things that don't matter, why be ashamed of having an arsehole, I stopped dieting, shaving, beating myself up, stopped waiting to talk, listened, felt pride, I stopped doing an impression of someone less nice than I really am.

I had to ban self-pity. Putting my leg on to begin with was hell, so when the pain got too much I'd think of things in my head that I'm grateful for dead quick.

'Teacoffeeswearingtoddlerswisdomjumblesalesmytattoosmyhair myfacemeandaboveallnurses, oooommmmmmm.'

The pain never went away, you see, it stayed, I can feel it in the leg that isn't there, phantom pain it's called, you know that muscle that you clench when you're trying to hold in a wee? Well, I can feel that on the sole of my phantom foot, and anything though goes in it.

Speaking of which. I did end up with Susan Matthews. She's very encouraging about me being a felt-tip weirdo. She doesn't buy blouses or grow her own herbs. She's normal – she eats Pot Noodle butties and worries about dogs she's only met once.

It's really weird that she only knew me for five minutes as two-legged me.

It's good, having your world turn upside down and owning it, I've got bigger balls now, you can't just have a shitty life and be expected to rise from it like the phoenix, the phoenix from the ashtray.

I *am* angry.

Do you want to see it? It is weird, you know when your nan drinks too much sherry at Christmas and takes her teeth out? Well… I could hide it away, that's what you do with ugly things that people are gonna judge you on, yeah could do that, or…

She takes her false leg off, removes stump sock – and draws on the stump.

Eh, Susan, I've got something to show yer! Are we on now for that threesome?

Laughter.

Fade to black.

THE SHED

Matilda Ibini

First performed by **Carly Houston**
as part of the BBC Studios Scotland production *CripTales*
on BBC America and BBC Four, directed by Jenny Sealey.

With thanks to Graeae Theatre Company
Dramaturg, April De Angelis

ANNETTE *takes a sip of some wine.*

Hey Julia, you're probably fast asleep, let me know what time it is when you get this... you might have noticed a different background, I'm filming from my kitchen, not the shed.

Sorry I missed recording last month's news, I broke our streak... before I forget, thank you for sending me that Tiger Balm, it really helped my muscle pain...

There's something I need to tell you...

You know how hard it is to recruit PAs, well I now employ five. I don't think I've ever had this many at any one time... To refresh your memory there's – Yasmeen, Clare, Ally, Simone, and Ellie; she's still in your old position, full time.

She's been with me – God, it'll be four years... I got good vibes about Ellie though, like she could last the distance. Ellie kept up your chore chart, she made sure all the other PAs did as well. She's a bit bossy, but she means well... She gets my chronic pain and she's so on it with my meds. She showed me how to be more productive and break down my projects into manageable tasks...

Don't tell anyone but... we even got drunk together one New Year's Eve. She makes me feel like more than just a monthly payslip, like you did... not that I'm comparing or anything. You know I would have you back in a heartbeat, if you ever decide to come back. I hope teaching's still going well.

I live next door to a teacher now, she moved in with her husband at the beginning of spring. I was writing in my shed when Ellie popped in.

'Your neighbour wants a word.'

I come out of the shed, and there she is, this smiley, curly redhead with a nose ring and bright eyes.

'Keira.'

She reached out her hand for a handshake but of course I can't reach it, so she picks up my hand in hers.

She invites me and Ellie to her housewarming barbecue, but their house isn't accessible, so Keira and Ellie take down two planks of wood from the fence between our gardens and I just managed to squeeze my wheelchair through.

I remember Ellie handing me a hotdog, with a smidge of mustard, and far too much ketchup. I take a bite (yuck) – Patrick, Keira's husband, says 'That's a veggie dog, better for the environment and your health... not your health specifically... everyone's – '

Keira offers me a beer; she opens it with her teeth... I ask for a straw.

'Afraid not, we're trying to limit our single-use plastics.'

'Is it really the humble straw that's polluting our oceans though?'

'Not, just straws, Ellie.'

'So what do you do for a living?'

She was talking to me. So I told her that I was a children's author and she seemed delighted.

Turns out she's a teacher, primary, she asked if I'd be up for doing a reading for the children in her nursery. Ellie butts in, 'She don't really do readings.'

Keira ignores this, she tells me that she can't pay me cos of budget cuts and all that but maybe, there's a skills-swap-thing that we can come to. Her piercing gaze pressures a 'sure' out of me.

You know how much time I spend in my shed... I love it to bits... and I love how it was made, Ellie, roped all the other PAs into making it for me for my birthday. They were probably too scared to say no... how they kept that a secret, I will never know... it's my sanctuary... so the day after I go in there to work, and there's a pack of recyclable straws taped to the door... moments later, there's a knock. I spin round and it's Keira.

'I hope you liked my peace offering.' She said, looking very pleased with herself, she'd came up with a way to pay me for the reading.

'I'll do up your garden.'

I like my unremarkable garden but Keira insists. She explains how she loves to tend to flowers and watch them evolve. She stresses that I shouldn't overlook my garden's potential. Then she gets down on her knees, puts her arm on my arm rest, 'Sometimes things just haven't had the chance to bloom.'

Then she does that intense-gaze thing again – pressures an 'okay' out of me... I really need to stop looking into her eyes...

She gives me her number. 'Send me some dates you're free, we'll grab a drink and discuss the reading?' As she leaves, Ellie comes in with my lunch. 'If you want your garden done up just say the word and I will.'

I had all I needed in my garden... my shed – besides, I'm in Operation Marathon mode to get book six completed... you remember my code names, right, for daily tasks and moods... My fave, Operation Sloth – PJ day; Operation Bush Control – my not-so-fave; Operation Rapunzel – hair-care days; and Operation Red Rum – painful days.

Funnily enough, Ellie seemed quite pained that I told Keira about our codes... I didn't really understand why, when Keira's been so lovely to the both of us. One afternoon when it was pissing it down Keira ran into the shed with a bottle of wine: 'Toasty. I can see why you like it in here.' She said as she filled my mug. She flicks through my books, I show her the marigold hidden in each one. I tell her about Mum, she loved marigolds.

The plan is to write thirteen picture books, one for each year we spent together – but Keira interrupts me with a kiss – and yes I know she's married... but it was one of those truly, earth-shaking, stars-exploding, clit-twitching kind of kisses – it rippled through me and for a moment all my aches and pains were silent.

I guess I've just been so used to being ignored that it surprised me that she didn't... I know that doesn't excuse what we did... and I know that it's wrong –

Honest to God, I tried to keep my distance, focus on my work but... then I hear grunts and shuffling from outside the shed. And there's Keira surrounded by sacks of soil, wooden boxes and pot plants.

'A deal's a deal, remember?'

Her face glistened with sweat as she poured soil into the boxes.

Ellie was not best pleased, she whispered to me, 'Seems like you've made a new friend by force or by fire. I'll tell her to go.'

'Could you get us some tea please, Ellie?'

Keira asks for a black coffee. Ellie rolls her eyes as she goes inside. Keira explains how she's got me some relatively easy plants to look after. A bit like me I say. She chuckles and then we sneak a snog behind the shed...

We stop as soon as we hear Ellie step out the kitchen. She comes round the shed with a mug in each hand. My heart's racing, my lips are throbbing, even my fingers tingled. Keira nurses her mug while Ellie feeds me sips of tea.

'Sorry, we've run out of straws. Are you wearing lipstick?'

Keira saves me.

'I put some on her. I thought the colour suited her.'

'Oh... Let's have a look then, I'll get you some next time I'm out.'

'I best be off.' Keira goes to leave.

'Mug?' Ellie demands.

Keira extends her arm to give the mug to Ellie but drops it before Ellie can reach it.

The mug doesn't break. Keira slips back through the gap in the fence. I drive into my shed.

Ellie follows, places the two incriminating mugs in front of me.

'What the fuck?...'

Then we have the biggest argument that we've ever had.

'You better stop whatever it is that's going on. You know she's just using you, right? If she really cared about you then she'd break up with Patrick. I'm only telling you this as a friend – '

'We're friendly, Ellie, but you're not my friend. I don't pay friends. She cares about me and I care about her...'

Ellie looks me dead in the face.

'Well... You can't have both of us. It's either me or her.' And then she walks off. She can't do that, can she?

Over the next few weeks Ellie is quieter than normal. I try to focus on my work but it's impossible, because all I can think about is Keira. It gets harder to be on my own around Keira, and then when she finishes the garden, she stops replying to my texts.

Ellie keeps switching and changing her shifts so I never know when to expect her. She fills the gap in the fence without telling me, she doesn't water my plants, she doesn't give me my pain meds any more unless I ask for them, and I'm pretty sure she hid the keys to the garden because Simone found them under the sink.

Then the most terrifying night of my life happened... Simone shook me awake in the middle of the night. She almost couldn't get me into my chair she was panicking so much...

...There was this glow pulsing through the kitchen window from the garden... it was my shed completely engulfed in flames...

My notebooks, months of work and research, first-edition copies of my published books, and worst of all I lost the only Polaroids of me and Mum.

Ellie visited me in hospital, she gave me these. She said, 'I made digital copies when I first built the shed, I just reprinted them.'

The fire brigade called the police who thought it was a hate crime because sheds don't exactly set themselves on fire. And whoever did it also vandalised the garden and threw a brick through the living-room window… I know that disability hate crime has risen over the years but I've lived here all my life and I've never had any trouble…

Why wouldn't they just throw the brick through the garden window?

Why go all the way round to the front… unless… unless they knew that's where the PAs sleep.

They wanted to wake them up. They wanted to ensure that Simone woke up.

But there's no CCTV, all the PAs' fingerprints are on the key safe to let themselves in, Ellie is the only one who knows how to change the code, she changed it after you left…

Ellie slipped up, she really slipped up. Look – (*At the Polaroid.*) this has a bend in the same place. These are my Polaroids. It's not exactly proof. I can't call the police. How would that make me look? Did she do what I think she did? How do I fire her without any evidence? Legally I have no grounds to.

What if she sues me? With my author's wage and benefits. She knows how much I earn, she knows the pin codes to my accounts. She knows all I have is this house that Mum left me. She knows…

ANNETTE *hears keys unlocking the front door.*

It's Ellie…

Fade to black.

HAMISH

Jack Thorne

First performed by **Robert Softley Gale**
as part of the BBC Studios Scotland production *CripTales*
on BBC America and BBC Four, directed by Amit Sharma.

In 1981, the electric wheelchair was available to purchase…
but not on the NHS.

HAMISH.

They'd done a radging meat raffle, done a stall at the fair, I saw
my poor old da standing in front of the tombola. Jar on the bar
for change when yer too pished to notice. Charity singalongs.
Non-school-uniform day at the school where my ma waves a
lollipop. They'd sold themselves again and again, trying like
shite to get the money together.

And it had come. Eight hundred and eight-five pounds of it,
plus ten pounds delivery.

My ma had this shit-licking grin on her face as the truck came
down the road. Neighbours standing in the road. Alan, Deirdre,
Blythe, Mark and bawbag Derek. International Year of
Disability and they'd given two pound to make themselves feel
a little bit less shite about the previous thirty-five.

There it is – the BEC-14 with speed control and direct rear-
wheel drive.

I'm loaded in and to whooping and applause I'm soon whizzing
up and down the street.

'How does it handle, Hamish?' 'Handles great, Da.' More
clapping.

But people are bored and turning away even as they do. That's
enough with the lad in the chair. He's had his moment. We've
had our two pounds' worth.

Then it's time for tea. Da goes back to his girlfriend's, me and
Ma linger, as is our way, and wash ready for bed. But like shite
am I doing that.

Thirty-six years I've needed someone to push me wherever I
needed to go.

Thirty-six years I've felt someone's breath on the back of my neck. Not tonight. I wait forty minutes, quiet as a mouse, takes some doing but then I'm out and I'm free. You don't get freedom like this on the NHS – the meat raffles have paid – and I am free. On the BEC-14.

Four miles an hour, midnight, wind in my hair, pass the house of Alan, Deirdre, Blythe, Mark and bawbag Derek. I've known them all, all my life. With their sorrowful looks towards my mother. I pass Mrs McGoonagh weaving down the street in her mini-skirt. 'Hello, pet,' I say.

She looks astonished. I know she'll tell my ma soon as soon as she sobers up. I don't care. Six miles per hour.

Ridgemount Hill. The wheels are screaming. I'm screaming.

YEEEEEAAAAAAHHHHHHHH!!!!

AAAAAAAAAAAAHHHHHHHHHH!

And there it is, laid out in front of me – Cratchit Woods.

It was something my ma used to talk about all the time, 'the dirty buggers at Cratchit Woods'. Got so I'd get hard every time I go past it at four o'clock on a Sunday. Just dreaming about the dirty buggers. And now I was going to be a dirty bugger.

This International Year, it has a slogan you cannae of missed if you watch a lot of Teletext as I do.

'See the ability not the disability.' Well, I've got one special ability, just one – eight wanks a day I managed, in 1973. Eight. Can cum on order, me – even with these bampot spades for hands!

The woods were dark, it was cold, I wasnae wearing my warmest coat, I was in a hurry to get what I need and leave. There's nobody here.

HELLO. Hello. Where is everyone?

I'm shivering. There's no one around. Hello.

I turn this. I turn that. I slip off the path. My wheels get stuck! Shit, shite, shit. Shite. Shite shite.

Here I am marooned like a jobby. Shit. Because here's the thing about the BEC-14. If a malfunction occurs in the drive-control system, a circuit breaker shuts off all power.

I look around. I look around. I look around. Where is everybody?

They're not bad parents. My ma says he left because of me, when she's pished. 'Could not for the life of him cope with dragging you around on a leash.' But other than that, they're not bad. Feel the love and all of that gash.

I came out to my ma. She said, 'Ah, that's fine, pet.' Came out to my da, he was like, 'Well I dunno what's possible, but if you want to have a go then you have a go.' He'd seen *The Naked Civil Servant*. That's all that he'd seen. And he thought – see the ability not the disability.

Nah, tongue my fart-box, you wallopers, you see me. I am the ability and the disability. I am Spasticus Autisticus. You see all of me. THIS IS WHAT I AM! SEE THIS!

HELP. HELP. HELP. I'm crying now.

He cautiously approaches. In his red jacket done up like he's concealing a weapon. He looks at me, I look back.

'Hello there, Hamish, bit stuck are you?'

'Yes, Derek, I am. What are you doing here?' I ask.

'Followed you.'

'Naw, you didnae.'

'Naw, you're right there, son.'

And suddenly bawbag Derek makes sense.

Forty minutes later. Me having got out the chair and laying on the floor like a shite. He finally manages to get it back on to the path and then he lifts me – tenderly – back into it. We try it and it goes. It's his idea to go back via the chip shop. He buys me a battered sausage and chips.

He asks me what I wanted down there. I say cock. He nods and says 'makes sense'.

I don't ask him what he wanted, I don't need to. I know. I ask him not to tell my ma. He says, 'Course not.' I ask him if he'll come out with me for chips again. He looks at me for a beat. Fifty years old. Out of shape in a red jacket that was past its best some time ago. 'Sure thing, kid.' He says.

We clean the wheels of my chair together. Then sort of go back to reality. He helps me in through the door of my house. My ma's light comes on but she doesn't come down.

'Can you get yerself to bed, kid?' he asks. 'I'm thirty-six years old, yes, I can.' He then nods. 'Chips sometime'll be good.' And just like that he's gone. The dirty bugger!

Managed nine wanks that night!

Fade to black.

THE REAL DEAL

Tom Wentworth

First performed by **Liz Carr**
as part of the BBC Studios Scotland production *CripTales*
on BBC America and BBC Four, directed by Ewan Marshall.

MEG *lives in a pristine shoebox. There is a window overlooking the street (where her phone sits on a tripod).*

MEG *sits in her wheelchair at her laptop, furiously typing time-coded entries into a benefit-fraud form.*

It was when he winked at me; I knew he had to be stopped. I'm not a snitch. But there comes a point and it's a sharp one – where you can't ignore things any longer.

Sniper-like, she spots something outside.

14:52. White Vest is back on the dot as usual. Say what you like about him (and I do), the one thing that I can't fault is his timekeeping.

(Lining up the shot. To her phone.) 'Shoot.'

'Shoot!' For God's sake.

It clicks.

Every day the same agonising performance: a slow, painful walk around the block with that stick of his. Every afternoon the same.

At 14:54 precisely he limps back into his house, pulling his trousers up over his (considerable) backside as he goes. I know a faker when I see one. We're all meant to be good little lambs tripping off to slaughter, but it's a criminal act we're talking about here. I simply can't let him get away with it.

Something catches her eye.

He's back out again. He never comes out at this time.

'Shoot.'

14:55. White Vest walking with stick. See, it's not even touching the ground, there's no weight on it at all. He's wearing a jacket over that vest of his. Going somewhere smart, are we?

Hm, if I didn't know better, I'd say someone was off to meet a lady friend.

MEG*'s doorbell rings. She freezes.*

Later. MEG *looks frail. Her wheelchair is gone.*

He looms over me like a shadow on stilts. Despite watching him day in, day out, we've hardly ever spoken. 'Alright,' he says, trying to make it sound casual.

'Yes, Mr Giles? Were you and your stick just passing?'

'Look, I know it's a big favour,' he says, gripping his stick tighter. And I wonder if he might strike me. 'But could I borrow your wheelchair?'

'It's broken, sorry.'

This isn't a lie, the battery's kaput, and I haven't had the energy to get another one. Some days I just can't be bothered. Rage and fatigue fight it out in my body, and the fatigue wins. Fatigue always wins.

White Vest comes straight back with, 'No problem. I can soon get it fixed up for you. What are neighbours for?'

I don't know what to do with my face, how I study the carpet intensely as he barges his way in. His eyes are gleaming now.

'Had my eye on one of these babies on the net for a while.' He says. 'But then I thought, why don't I go and see my old friend Sue.'

'Meg,' I correct him. 'But my name's Miss Davies.' White Vest plays with a bit of mucus on his finger as he studies my chair and me in it.

'I can soon get her fixed up. Even got a battery at home. Just don't ask what lorry it fell off.'

I want to shout, 'Look here, Mr Giles. My wheelchair is not a "baby"! It's functional. To get me from one place to another.'

But before I even realise what's happened White Vest has literally taken my chair from under me.

'You're a brick, Sue!' he says.

'Good thing I came over isn't it? Your knight in shining armour.'

Bloody cheek.

'You haven't said why you want it,' I say.

'Did I not mention?' White Vest tries to look innocent. 'I've got my face-to-face PIP assessment tomorrow and well, you gotta up your game, haven't you?' He lets the word 'assessment' fizz like a tablet dropping in water.

God, I need some painkillers.

My whole body burns. 'But you don't need a wheelchair,' I say.

'Not at the moment,' he says dramatically, 'but in a year, who knows? They don't know how degenerative this condition of mine might be.'

I feel sick.

'I'll bring it back,' he shouts, pushing it down the drive. 'A deal's a deal.'

'Thank you,' I call, as if he's done me the favour. Why the hell did I say thank you?

Beat.

White Vest makes me feel like they did at the assessment centre. From the moment the X-Ray-eyed receptionist smiled at me, I knew I'd lost. I tried so hard to look capable; smart, even though I felt like an imposter. When my letter arrived, I knew what it said without opening it…

'Just be yourself, Meg. Sit tall. Smile.' My mother's voice comes through, as always. But as I sit there I think of how it was because I attended her funeral that I lost my benefits. I chose her over them. And now I'm paying for it.

Of course, X-Ray Eyes sees right through me. My guilt. The fact that I felt I didn't deserve it.

For hours the night before I made a list of all the things I couldn't do and in the morning I felt worthless.

I held it tightly in my hand, but the more questions they asked me, the more my hand went into spasm and the paper crumpled. I crumpled.

Later. MEG*'s back at her desk again, holding her PIP letter…*

The next day you-know-who is back, zooming down the road, running down my new battery.

'King of the road, me!' He shouts from the street, like a pitbull with two tails. I want to punch those yellow teeth of his as he jumps nimbly from my wheelchair. There's not a shred of decency in the man.

I brandish my assessment letter at him. 'Look!' I shout. 'It's so bloody unfair. I go to them, and they give me nothing, you go to them, they hand it to you on a plate. Just leave me alone.'

He lands on the assessment letter like a hungry vulture. And for the first time, I see a genuine light shining in his eyes. 'You can appeal,' he said. I feel all the air go out of me like a deflated balloon. 'It's so humiliating,' I say.

'You have to fight.' White Vest grabs me by the shoulders. 'You know your trouble: you simply don't look disabled enough.'

My jaw hits the floor.

'You dress too smart.'

'I have my pride!' I shout, but he just shakes his head.

'And where's pride ever got you?'

Without warning, he waltzes in and starts rummaging through my dirty-washing basket.

I desperately try to stop him as bras and knickers fly but finally, he holds up my oldest, dirtiest blouse.

'This is the one,' he says, salivating like a huge, horny Doberman.

'Wear this to your next assessment, and they'll never be able to turn you down.'

Then White Vest tips the whole basket onto the floor, going through it like a like a pig searching for truffles.

Out comes some sweatpants I'd wet myself in last week and hadn't been able to wash.

'Lovely,' he says, smelling the crotch.

She rubs her hands with antibacterial gel at the memory.

What White Vest is suggesting is terrible. Horrible. Wrong…

But they are my clothes, after all.

I mean, it's not exactly lying.

Stop it, Meg. Don't even think of it. But in that terrible moment, I just know… White Vest is right.

Beat.

'You need to be more disabled!' he shouts at our daily training session.

'I am disabled!' I screamed in his face (and I felt it).

'I don't think you really want this,' he said. I wanted to forget I even existed. I could feel my old friend fatigue taking over, and White Vest was ready to take full advantage.

While MEG *speaks as White Vest, we see her turn into what he describes.*

'Don't sit tall. Slump.'

'Dribble a bit. Aw, they love that.'

'Slump more. More. Look pained.'

'Look vacant. Don't shake hands.'

'No make-up. No sleep the night before. Now you're the real deal. But most important of all, don't speak. I'll do all the talking.'

The easiest part of White Vest's plan was the not sleeping. By going blithely along had I made myself exactly like him? A good little lamb to the slaughter...

Later. MEG *sits at her desk with a bottle of fizz and two glasses. She has a few blurry shots of White Vest pinned up on the wall, like an incident room.*

White Vest told a pack of lies, of course. But they believed every word that came from his silver tongue.

'No, Miss Davies can't wipe her own arse.'

'No, Miss Davies can't fold her own sheets.'

'No, Miss Davies can't cook a meal.'

'Miss Davies can't stand up, sit down, or do the Hokey Cokey.'

'Don't you understand, Miss Davies couldn't even open the envelope your letter arrived in.'

When we got out, we celebrated. Actually we celebrated all afternoon.

White Vest even bought me champagne – okay, it's cheap supermarket stuff, but I'm not complaining. When it was time for him to go I said, 'Mr Giles, thank you.' And he said, 'Call me Nigel.'

She smiles. Drains her glass.

And then he winked at me again. That was your mistake, Nigel. You've made me see things clearer than I have done for weeks... You've made me feel alive again... You've reminded me that you can't get away with it and that I am the real deal.

We see MEG *submit the benefit-fraud form. She smiles.*

Fade to black.

**BBC Studios Scotland
in association with BBC America**

Written, directed and performed by disabled people

Script Supervisor	JEMMA FIELD
Production Coordinator	SOPHIE RICHARDSON
First Assistant Director	HELEN OSTLER
Floor Runner	ETHOSHEIA HYLTON
Art Director	LIZZIE BARDWELL
Standby Art Director	SARA HAYWARD
Production Buyer	KATYA GUY
Prop Master	DAVE BROCK
Dressing Props	MARK SIMPSON
Standby Props	PAUL WHALE
BSL Interpreters	CHANDRIKA GOPALAKRISHNAN
	NATALIE McDONALD
	SOPHIE ALLEN
	VIKKI GEE DARE
Costume Supervisor	BECCI MARKS
Focus Puller	MURAT AKYILDIZ
Camera Assistant	LEA AUBIGNE
Jib Operator	NEIL IRWIN
	JOE McNALLY
	ARUN TAYLOR
Jib Technician	CHRIS COLE
DIT	JAMES ENGLAND
Gaffer	JASON CLARE
Best Boy	WERNER VAN PEPPEN
Electrician	MORGAN GOODSMITH
Boom Operator	SEAN HENNESSY
Graphics	SERIOUS FX
Dubbing Mixer	ADAM WOOD
Colourist	BEN MULLEN

Online Editor	GORDON MILLER
Sound Recordist	IAN CURRIE
Make-up Designer	GARY JORDAN
Costume Designer	LIBBY IRWIN
Production Designer	ALISON BUTLER
Director of Photography	JONO SMITH
Editor	LINDY CAMERON
Production Manager	FRANCES KILGOUR
Production Executive	LISA PHELAN
Commissioner for the BBC	LAMIA DABBOUSSY
Executive Producer	DEBBIE CHRISTIE
Creative Director	MAT FRASER

© BBC MMXX

Author Biographies

Genevieve Barr

Genevieve Barr is a deaf writer and actor from Harrogate. After reading History and English Literature at the University of Edinburgh, Genevieve taught at a secondary school in South London before her breakout performance in the lead role in *The Silence* for the BBC. As a writer, Genevieve won the Red Planet Prize in 2020 and has original series commissions with ITV and Channel 4. She has also co-written a single drama for the BBC with Jack Thorne. As an actor, Genevieve is also known for her roles in BBC's *Press* and *Call the Midwife*, BAFTA-winning series *The Fades*, ITV's *Liar* and Channel 4's *Shameless*. She most recently starred alongside Sarah Lancashire in Channel 4's *The Accident*, which became the highest-rated drama premiere of 2019.

Mat Fraser

Mat Fraser is an internationally known disabled actor, writer and musician, whose writing has sometimes been awarded. His solo show *Cabinet of Curiosities: How Disability Was Kept in a Box* won the UK's Observer Ethical Award for Arts & Entertainment in 2014, and he wrote the ONEOFUS production of *Jack & The Beanstalk*, for which the *New York Times* awarded him and his director/performer wife Julie Atlas Muz 'New Yorkers of the Year' in 2018. Mat is thrilled to curate this series of monologues around disability, *CripTales*, for BBC America and BBC 4, also writing and acting in one of the pieces. Mat believes that authentic disabled voices are vital in the telling of disability stories, and everything he writes has a connection to disability. He's (usually!) currently working on a TV drama and a stage play.

Jackie Hagan

Jackie Hagan has council-estate bones and an odd number of limbs. She is a Jerwood Compton Poetry Fellow and has won the Saboteur Award for Best Spoken Word Show in both 2016 and 2018 for her solo shows. She is also a bisexual amputee who downs champagne from her glittery false leg and dresses her stump up as celebrities in her stand-up/cabaret act. She has toured the UK extensively and has most recently performed at The Secret Policeman's Ball at The Palace, Manchester, Cripping the Arts Festival in Toronto and at The Slipper Room, New York. When she made the move from solo shows to plays, she was taken on Graeae Theatre Company's Write-to-Play scheme and ultimately they and Manchester's Royal Exchange co-produced her play *Cosmic Scallies* in 2017. She co-founded and ran a not-for-profit organisation for twelve years, providing creative workshops, support and opportunities for isolated adults, and has delivered over two thousand creative workshops for LGBTQ groups, youth clubs, and one-on-one work with many emerging artists, often facing similar adversity regarding disability and class. She tours with Fantabulosa! as her alter ego, Freya Bentos, in a drag show about gender aimed at three-to-eight-year-olds that is performed in any open-air situation. Jackie leads LGBTQ equality training. She is passionate about making theatre accessible and her children's Christmas play (Contact Theatre, Manchester, in 2019 and 2021) was called 'meticulously accessible' by *The Stage*. She has CRPS, a pain disorder that means she is in constant severe pain; she's trying to learn from it, but mainly she has learnt that is okay to put a blanket over your head and have a big cry.

Matilda Ibini

Matilda Ibini is an award-winning bionic playwright and screenwriter. She is a writer on Sphinx Theatre's 30 Project and is English Touring Theatre's writer for their Nationwide Voices programme. Credits include *Unprecedented* (Headlong/Century Films/BBC4), *Little Miss Burden* (Bunker Theatre), *The Grape That Rolled Under the Fridge* (BBC Radio 3), *Choice and Control* (Old Vic Theatre), *Muscovado* (UK tour). Her work has been staged at Shakespeare's Globe, Bush Theatre, Soho Theatre, Arcola Theatre, Hackney Showroom and VAULT Festival. She has a number of screen projects in development with production companies.

Jack Thorne

Jack Thorne writes for television, film and theatre. He is also a proud member of the disabled community. Being asked by Mat to write for this was a dream; getting to write for Robert (an actor he's long been obsessed by), and have it directed by the great Amit was even dreamier.

Tom Wentworth

Tom Wentworth's recent credits for theatre include *Burke and Hare* (Watermill/Jermyn Street), *Bully* (recipient of an MGCFutures Bursary and performed at Wales Millennium Centre), *Bee Happy* (Old Red Lion) and *Windy Old Fossils* (Pentabus). He's currently under commission to National Theatre Wales. *Windy Old Fossils* and *Burke and Hare* are published by Fair Acre Press. For television, Tom's delighted to have contributed to *CripTales*. He is developing original work across radio and television, as well as across the BBC's continuing drama series, and has recently been a part of BBC Writersroom's London Voices and Writers Access Group for emerging disabled talent.